MW01247053

Maci Terry is an artist and writer from Oklahoma City.

Her love for poetry began at age 12, in a small pocket notebook –
since then, the art of poetry has enveloped Maci's life.

Through her musings, she writes to create connection and inspire
vulnerability in the hearts of others. *Bloom* is the author's first
published book – a collection of her earliest pieces.

To

the ones

blooming

Maci Terry

BLOOM

AUSTIN MACAULEY PUBLISHERS™

LONDON • CAMBRIDGE • NEW YORK • SHARJAH

Ordering Information
Quantity sales: Special discounts are available on quantity purchases by corporations, associations, and others. For details, contact the publisher at the address below.

Publisher's Cataloging-in-Publication data
Terry, Maci
Bloom

ISBN 9781649795458 (Paperback)
ISBN 9781649795465 (ePub e-book)

Library of Congress Control Number: 2022921211

www.austinmacauley.com/us

First Published 2023
Austin Macauley Publishers LLC
40 Wall Street, 33rd Floor, Suite 3302
New York, NY 10005
USA

mail-usa@austinmacauley.com
+1 (646) 5125767

To my Abba
who gave me the
heart to craft these words.

To Mom and Dad,
your support waters my flowers.

To those who have walked with me,
pushed me, and celebrated with me –
thank you.

Table of Contents

To Begin

"Fill your paper with the breathings of your heart."
William Wordsworth

Bloom is My young heart, open and exposed.
My deepest desire to come from this book is for you
to read these pages and know that you are seen.
Every single moment –
every laugh, every tear, every smile, every heartbreak –
and all of what's in between is written here.
As you read, remember
with every single breath, you are flourishing into
who you are created to be.
I hope *Bloom* inspires
you to grow towards love and light,
it's where you're meant to be.

Maci

PART ONE

SOW

First Words

When you sneak up into my mind
ambivalence follows close behind.
Everything you are
all we could be
you don't even realize who you are to me.

Decide

You
are
worth
more

                                       but
                                       you
                                    aren't
                                     worth
                                           me.

Memories

When it comes down to it,
it's only time.
A laugh,
a smile,
a glance,
a dance.
A fall,
a step,
a hand,
a chance.
Now, it's gone.
You'll never read that for the first time again.
It's a memory.
We can always relive the memories,
but we can never live them again.

Misconstrue

She doesn't know what she has,
but you don't know what you're missing.

Even When You Don't Feel It

Even on your worst days
never forget
to show kindness
because kindness
was shown first to you.

Ethereal

Oh,
to glance at the stars
and see the heavens
is truly glorious.

Unrequited Love

For you could never
return the feelings I have for you,
but I'd still stand before you
and say that
I love you.

Feelings

You lied,
deceived,
cheated,
questioned,
fooled,
I never knew my heart could play such a game.

If They Knew

Her.
I never should have fallen for you
I never should have let you in
never should have given myself
a chance to love again
I never should have wished you'd call
I never should have tried
never should have made a move
that would have made me cry.

Him.
I never should have let her fall
I never should have left her then
never should have broken the chance
to love her once again
I never should've doubted to call
I never should have lied
I never should have made that move
that would have made her cry.

3 A.M.

When did my feelings return?
How could I have known?
Why didn't I decide to leave my heart alone?
Constantly playing tug a war,
battling to win
when will my heart ever learn
not to let you in?
All you'll do is break it
slowly, piece by piece
and worst of all,
you don't even know you have a hold on me.

Immeasurably More

I dream of high things
the possibility of adventure
uncertainty of the future
certain of the past
always focused on the one
who already knows my path
he guides my feet
he holds my hand
knowing what is promised
will continue to stand

Fall in grace,
rise with love.

Freedom

You are happiest
when you aren't trying to be.

Hard Truth

The only way to love you

                                        is from a distance.

But Now

Give me a sunset,
I see the strokes of an artist
give me heartbreak,
I see healing hands
give me disaster,
I see hope peaking
give me hatred,
I see love glimmering
give me this world,
I see Jesus.

Fields

Trying to describe
the way I feel about you
is telling me to pick
one flower out of a field
and defining why it is
my absolute favorite.

Highlights

The brightness of it all
can suck us in
I see at the table
over there, right by them
the couples stare
the children gawk
it almost seems as if
everyone's in awe.
I don't aspire to be like them,
consumed by a screen
I dream to be living
everyday pursuing my dreams
unbothered by trends
by like or posts,
but concerned with my heart
and the pursuit of its growth.
No, I don't want to be seen just behind a screen.

Flood

You never know when the words
will come to flow.
As a river flooding when it rains,
it comes suddenly, running through my veins
something stirs the water
the waves rising up to shore
free fallin' on the radio, dancing in the car mindlessly
and maybe I don't make sense,
but the feeling of a writer never does.
So when there's a pressing in your heart,
words wishing to escape,
grab a pen.

Oxygen

Our minds so narrow
we hate on hate,
when the only way to kill a fire
is to cut off the oxygen.
Hate on hate will only create a forest fire.
Kill hate
with love
with love
with love
with love.

You Are His

The creator of the Earth
the moon, the stars
wants his dearest creation –
you.
Oh, do you realize
how many times we turn away?
And hand in hand,
here he stands
patiently waiting
for his child to come home.
He calls you by name,
he calls you by heart,
so step into the light
and
out of the dark.

Saturday Morning

You feel like Saturday morning
fresh and calm
up for anything
cozy and clueless
unpredictably knowing
pushing for more
and waiting to see.

Canvas

The whole sky
could be my canvas
and it wouldn't be
enough to express
how I feel about
those gold speckled eyes,
the strokes of your hand in the dim light,
a blank page made to turn
something I've always been waiting for.

How Do I Fight What I Do

You don't owe me anything
neither I do you
yet
somehow I feel
I have to,
I need to,
I must
save you.

Hopeless Romantic

Chivalry
the absence of text
phone calls and door bells
kisses in the rain
drive in movies, star gazing
these things fill my brain
slowness
going steady
handwritten letters
opened doors and held hands
classic music,
scenic routes down the roads
call me old fashioned,
too far gone
but I'll be the first to say
that I will endlessly
wait for the one.

Burn

I'm sorry
I forgot how to heal
I take every emotion
and try to make it real.
Every thought I must keep
none left behind
but once I write it down
it haunts inside my mind
take them away
throw them in the fire
I'm sorry,
I forgot how to heal
I threw you in the fire
and quickly pulled you out,
but you've already burned.
let me heal you
let me bandage your wounds
I never meant for the flames
to get a hold of you.

Trust

You say the word "trust"
like it's something you can lend
but once you take it away,
seldom can I give.

Blind Eyes

Ordinary times become
extraordinary moments,
all we have to do is
open our eyes to the wonder and beauty
surrounding us.

Writing

I cannot be held back
I must release
give away parts of my soul
for the good in me
I need expression,
feelings defined
I can never stop
it aches my heart
I can't let go, I'll lose control.

Collide

Maybe
you and I
are just too far apart
maybe
you and I
collide far too hard.

Being Vulnerable Isn't Easy, But

Vulnerability is beautiful
vulnerability is kind
vulnerability is clarity
vulnerability is warmth
vulnerability is comfort
vulnerability is uncomfortable
vulnerability is truth
vulnerability is trust
vulnerability is needed
vulnerability is important
vulnerability is love
vulnerability is heart filled
vulnerability is mindful
vulnerability is soulful
vulnerability is hard
vulnerability is worth it
vulnerability is everything.

Sea of Lovers

Admire me from afar
and I shall you
in the sea of lovers drowned
let's enjoy the view.

Lost

I am lost now in the starlight
I see black and white when you're shining so bright
the wind blows the ground shakes
no movements can I make
the moon glows
the sun dims
you have turned my galaxy into a virtuous whirlwind.

Garden

The prettiest flowers
you picked out of the garden
planted not for you.
now the remains,
the weeds grown in
on the place love once lived.

Hidden Sin

It sneaks up my heart
bubbles through my veins
it binds my hands
leaving me estranged
I see only dark, flashes of red
my ears can no longer hear
I only feel dread
yes, it takes a lot of me
to overcome jealousy.

Life

Then there's music to match the memory, and every time I glance back,
I look at the magic in all the little moments.
In the small glances, the passing seconds.
These pockets of joy have made up a little thing called life.

Distance, Distant

When words fail
and I am far
feel my love
I'm sending you
from here.

True Love

The best love is
unfathomable
reckless
forgiving
graceful
overflowing
unconditional
kind
remarkable
indescribable
the best love is
Jesus.

Your Heart Is My Heart

It hurts my heart
breaks me down
I feel your pain
but I cannot imagine it
the burdens you carry
the sadness you face
for if it happened to me,
could I sustain?
I can't understand
somehow I shouldn't
but I know one thing:
it shouldn't be you.

Shock

It's not happening
this cannot be real
everything that's happened
and this is how you feel?
The number of hearts broken
there can't be many more
pretty soon we'll all be left
with them shattered on the floor.

This Love

There is no greater love
I break his heart
but he,
but he
loves me just the same
all my mistakes, all my regrets
wash away like rain.

Love Language

Just say the words
let me know
actions speak louder
only if you've spoken at all.

Agape

How beautiful love is
when it is seen.

Time

Believe me when I say, hold onto precious time. Do not let the little moments slip through the cracks because the smallest slots of time will make up the biggest spaces in your heart.

I Don't Know

I speak
but no words come
I think
but no thoughts form
I love
but don't know how.

Real

Have you ever wondered
what it would be like
if we said what we thought?
The time we'd save
the places we'd go
if you just told me
what's in your brain?
Tell me what's real.

Wreck of Our Hearts

Yesterday's conversation
today's miscommunication
a piece is gone,
drifted afar
all we're left with
the wreck of our hearts.

Who Am I to Be

A valley

      bow to my king

a mountain

      rise to my creator's call

a wave

      pulled towards his tide

a rock

      firmly standing by his side.

Something to Hold Onto

I don't have a memory,
nor a moment
give me something more
than a fleeting emotion.

Rise

Perhaps the most fascinating yet enduring things
is the fact that
every single day when you rise,
you will undoubtedly create a new day
one that has never been lived before, one that will never be
lived again.

Two Different, Too Different

The words in your head
thoughts in your heart
both, they seem
too far apart.

PART TWO

RAIN

I Know How You Feel

I just want you to know:
The thoughts that you keep,
in that cold dark place
the ones that creep in
and make you feel unsafe
the thoughts that you would die
to admit, but you never will
those lonely, scared thoughts
can be brought into the light,
you can heal.

What Is Familiar

I'm sorry if you can't see me straight
the only way my heart is taught
is through all these games
deceptive and deceiving
insecurity always draws near
so forgive my walls and natural reply,
my heart has been fooled
one too many times.

Lonely Dance

The only capable
is far unattainable
swaying with me,
looking to her.
Peek in my heart
and you might see –
you're the only one
really consuming me.

You Don't Need Me

Open your eyes
can't you see?
The insecurity I feel
is slowly surrounding me
every single time
everywhere I go
never enough
always second choice
and they joke as they wonder
can't you see?
You question why I'm guarded
I'm nothing more to you
than you are to her
so please stop now
you won't understand
I cannot begin to speak
the emotions have set in
I'm through with the comparison
the endless mind game
if your decision is so hard,
if it's not clear to see
then I'll make it for you –
you don't need me.

In My Mind

Why do I feel the way I feel
why do I think the way I do
why do I say the things I say
but never say them to you?

Important

You've heard it enough, let me say it again
it has nothing to do with you
and everything to do with them.

Nostalgia

What a feeling
lost and at home
content and dissatisfied
joyful and sad
full and empty.

Beauty of Girls

Maybe that's the beauty of girls.
So strong
so independent
so brave
so caring
so outspoken
yet
so fragile
so small
so heartbroken
so tender
yes, your heart is bigger than your head.
And that's beautiful.

Calling

I
don't
want
to
live
in
the
bondage
of
this
world
I
want
to
live
in
the
freedom
of
your
love.

Please Let Me In

I can't help it
I can't help my heart
as it breaks
because you won't open up yours
so here's mine,
spilling out
and you,
watching it fall.

With Me

I hope you know –
every letter you write
every word you speak
every gesture you make
I keep it in my heart
and carry it with me.

Once

That feeling
whisked away
but that tune
begins to serenade my heart
I start to swing
and sway
as my mind
takes me back
to that night,
that wonderful time.

Touch

At some point you look up
and you see
all the people in your life
who have shaped you
tested you
loved you
hated you
forgave you
trusted you
and there they are
then they're moving on
and this is what life is about
the people you touch
and the ones who touch you back.

Flesh and Bone

My soul fights
what God offers freely
peace is right on the edge of the horizon,
but I long to hold on to these offenses and regrets,
mulling over them as if they add anything to my life
it doesn't raise my status higher.
I am the lowest, the lord is the highest.
The lord is the
only one
to raise me up.

Right Here

So many of us wonder,
when will my life begin?
You're living, you're breathing
aren't you?
Life is now.
There's not a certain point when everything changes
it's not when you get a car, when you graduate,
when you turn 18, when you get married.
It's already started.
It began when your heart started beating.
Your life has already begun.
but new life,
new life.
new life begins the second you decide to follow Jesus,
and take into account what a blessing each day truly is.
Right now – life is here.
Jesus is in the present.
we don't know what is to come
Jesus is in the present.
he wants us to live a life of wonder, a life of love
but he wants us to live it right now.

The extraordinary is hard to find in the seemingly
ordinary, but it's there.
Life is a precious gift, chosen by our
Heavenly Father.
Time even more, treat it as such. Live in the now.

Unspoken Hues

That night it seemed
the sky spoke
the unsaid hues of our hearts
the warm golden hour
the pink streaks of light
clouds intertwined in it all
welcoming the night
that moment in my head
forever ours to keep
it's locked inside my heart
safe, where it should be.

A Shift

I can't explain what happened
or when my feelings changed
I've become a different person
one without those chains
my feelings don't bind me,
you can walk right by me
I don't have to say a word,
I know I won't be heard.

Complicated Game

My heart and my head
the two worst enemies
friends for a moment
the extremity of views
one is explosions of yes,
one is poundings of no
I don't know which way to go
they've become intertwined.
I say what I think,
but don't know what I feel
I feel what I think
but don't know what is real.
Confusing completely,
I try to explain
but can't say anything.
This by far,
the most complicated game.

Family

Of
all the
somebodies to
call
one of my own
happily, I will say
a family is
here,
always.

Lost

It wasn't intentions
misguided prevention
trying to steer the boat
only going the wrong way
the storm is moving in
the rafts are closing shut
no way out
only through the crashing sea
you'll never find me.

Just You

I have never met you
your inspiration
your warmth
you make everyone feel like someone
I'm not poetic
but the way you live is
how much hardship you face
and how much love you give
you write it down
line it on your heart
all the beauty I see
has shone since the start
so thank you
for your immovable mark
for the perspective you shared
I am changed,
utterly and completely.

Turning Page

Kicking myself now
for unknown then
you looked at me once
I threw the towel in
you've yet to leave my mind
all my memories
far behind
you've filled every blank space
now all I'm left with –
a turning page.

Poetry

My heart is filled
when I capture the feeling
because for me,
poetry
is all the words
I couldn't say
all the emotions
I couldn't feel
all the thoughts
I couldn't think.

Road Less Traveled

I've never been down this road
though I know which way to go.

How Do You See

All I want is for you to see me in your light.

Tired

I'm tired of falling for you
when you've never tripped over me.

Sun Ray

You are sunshine raining down
drops of golden, drops of light
you grow towards love
you grow towards grace
my heart is open
you have mended it
my spirit is filled
alive is all I am
when you're with me
inspiration and creativity
of the unseen flows from your lips
as I sit in amusement
of all your rays
I feel the streaks of light and urgency of now
and you have opened a door
that no one can close.

Greatest Fear

As I saw you in the distance
standing alone
you looked like a shadow
no place to call home
that's when it came
my epiphany in view
my greatest fear
is to ever leave you.

Family Ties

She's gone
He's away too
They're lost,
and here I am.
I'm here.
Stranded between these disconnected seas
without knowing which way to swim,
I'm already drowning.

Let Me Listen

The fact that
I won't understand
portrays the single idea
that what you have to say
is what you don't want me to hear.
Let me try to understand,
for this pre-notion of misconception has already driven us
apart.

Behind Your Eyes

Behind your eyes
I see what I don't want to hear
and all I want to know
behind your eyes
I see the truth of your light
and the darkness in mine
behind your eyes
I see my past untied
and our future to bind
but behind your eyes
I see every fear begin
all my doubts, beginning to end.

Time After Time

Time and time again
I let you in to see
a different side of me
you'd never thought I'd be
and time and time again
fooled by what makes sense
standing in the rain
tears roll down my face
I wanna walk away
you just stay the same
leave me here alone
leave me here to be
I wanna be free
needing time to heal
separating what is real
what is real?

Know Me

Tell me when I laugh the hardest
tell me when I cry the most
tell me what you see in my eyes
and what you couldn't bear without
tell me how my hand feels in yours
tell me every single doubt
tell me what you love of me
what you wish would never change
tell me how your heart skips a beat
if I ever say your name
tell me how you knew it was me
everything you see
tell me anything you've thought of
tell me how you love me.

Change

A lot of things change in a year
but my feelings never did.
Looking back now, I'm wondering how
how could I feel so much for just an idea?
An illusion?
I've led myself this far
without the knowledge of why
everyday spent in melancholy
over someone I didn't even want.

If You Don't

If you don't love me anymore
don't spare my feelings
don't lie to me.
Just yesterday
you were in over your head
and I was just beginning to feel it too.
Then your mind changed, your heart raced
commitment was too much it seemed,
but I still wish you didn't lie to me.

Yours

Once again God
you show me what I'm worth
you gently unravel me
into the arms that are yours
my shame falls to the floor
all I am,
all I ever wanna be is yours

In Love with a Feeling

I'm not in love with a person
in love with a feeling,
filled with countless reasons
to keep on believing
deep in my soul
I seem to understand
we're not made for each other
but we're hand in hand
easily my heart could break
as well as yours could hurt
false positives have led us astray,
with no idea where to turn.

Unsaid and Unseen

All you never said
was everything I heard
filling in the gaps
with the holes in your words.
I danced upon the maybes
lived in the unknown
my heart came out torn
from the promises you'd sworn.

A Moment

Mindlessly twirling to dancing queen,
singing our hearts out.

How?

Undeserving,
yet you carried my cross.
You carried my shame,
and still call me by name.

I Wish

You don't ask why I write,
but I wish you would.
You don't see when I smile,
but I wish you could.
You don't wonder where I am,
but I wish you did.
I can't let you go,
but I bet you can.

Misused and Confused

Many come and go
no one ever stays
I wish you could understand
I'm tired of feeling this way.

Cycles

I'm reminded again
of all I don't have
and everything I'm afraid of
just another, just the same
taken for granted
always stuck in my shame
I know you'll be different
but I hope to see something different
inside you, inside me.

Seasons

You make the night loud.
you make the stars shine,
so bright to meet my eyes
you make the earth turn,
the gravity sweeps my feet
you make the wind blow,
all the autumn leaves
trickling down on me
you make the snow fall,
the chillness of winter
making me numb
you make the flowers bloom,
from the rays of sun
you make my days into nights,
you make my nights into life.

Which Me

You've only seen the old me
I'm afraid to show you what I've come to be
I'm changing every second
the speed of light
wishes to catch up to the beat of my heart.
Will you see me?
Will you love me?
Or will you reject the new, and expect the old?

My Vow

Eagerness has always drawn near
and it lingers, still
but the peace I have
has taken up space
with the thought of your soon to be place
my heart has a spot for you,
and I solemnly promise
to keep the spot for you
and only you,
hoping this promise will soon come true.

High Hopes

I was naive to think
removing you from my heart would be so easy
I'm done, we're through
were the words I uttered
until you entered my view
it all came back, the feelings so familiar
the old became the new,
everything I forgot soon remembered
swallow my feelings, swallow my pride
you walk right by me,
left with no surprise.

Atlas

The vastness in view
the wondrous skies
you have traveled many valleys
overcome many hills.
even more so,
your compass shifts
into your ever-growing midst
look not only at what you've done
imagine what you can do.

Go

There are far too many
books to read
people to meet
chances to take
lessons to learn
movies to watch
places to see
adventures to explore
to not, my friend.

PART THREE

SUN

Once

Where has the magic gone?
the sweetness of its kind.
somewhere it got left along,
somewhere far behind.
I try to recapture its tenderness
the music in our days
needing a flame to rekindle
what once was ablaze.

I Wish I Didn't

Was it too much to ask for you to care?
For you to hurt for me? Was I not enough?
Was I never enough?
I walked out of your life, you never blinked twice
all the memories we shared, all the things we did
and I'm not even worth a second glance.

Vs. Action

"I love you."
"I love you."
"I'm so sorry for hurting you."
These words repeat in my mind,
as your actions never amount up to your words
how can you say one thing
and repeatedly treat me the same?
You can't criticize me
when you're also to blame.
You hurt, you lie
I don't know what to believe
catch yourself before you speak
'others keep hurting you'
when you're only hurting me.

Demons

I try, I try, I try
all I feel is hurt
the pain swells up inside me
I can never explain the way it burns.
I think it's okay
no, I'm fine, it'll heal
yet I come back into this place
and none of that is real.
I was gentle, can't you see?
You're inflicting the pain
the burden bound to me.
We were in a good place,
and you let him win again.
How many times will you shut me out,
and let the demons in?

You Are What They Are Not

I have to remind myself –
you are limitless;
and my problems are not
you are omniscient;
and my problems are not
you are the outcome;
and my problems are not
you are the answer;
and my problems are not.

Running

My mind running into my heart –
it's outrunning itself.
Hate is running from love –
love is running to heal.
Healing is running to pain –
pain is running from grace.
Grace is running to anger –
anger is running from peace
peace is running to you,
while I am running from me.

Fill Me

My lungs could exhale all their breath
and I could never sing enough
my feet could walk for miles
and I could never tell enough
my heart could beat a million times
and never love enough
no,
no measure amounts to you.

In My Mind

These words come into my brain
with no place to put them
these thoughts retrieve my mind
and I cannot take them
these actions are seen
but never believed
these people,
they love you.
But you don't love me.

You'll Never See the Full Story from One Side

Perspective changes everything.

Ode to You

It's not for me
you're not for me
I was fooled by you
never thought I knew
you weren't for me
no, not for me
I was left outside
cold and dark and dry
take it back
oh, take it back
those endless nights
your eyes like mine
it's not for me
you're not for me
I was lost in you
never thought I knew
you weren't for me
no, not for me
here I am right now
trying to turn around
take me back
oh, take me back
I want those endless nights

your eyes close to mine
you're right for me
you're right for me
never thought I knew
I was right for you.

Falling, Falling

I won't pretend to be something I'm not
I'm not a poet
I'm closer to the edge
farther from you
I'm not yours
nor will I ever be
I'm used to being seen
only imaginarily
the ghost of me
has covered it all
backing down
before I fall
without you near
to succumb to the grounds
I've welcomed all my fears
I've been here before
unreturned promises
here I stand
desperately waiting
an outstretched hand
just your hand
a soft place to land.

Ache

Every word not from you
left unread
digging a deeper hole
tears of more shed
please take this away
this ache in my heart
my bones are shaking
you're tearing me apart.

The Best of Me

I took for granted every moment spent with you
glanced over and gone, as I walk right on through.
"You don't know what you have until it's gone,"
But I know what I had
still, you're gone.
Where did the time go?
How short are the days?
You were here before
and I wish it was the same
the piece of my heart
that you held is now gone
you took it
you have it
time got the best of us,
and you got the best of me.

How Long Has It Been Since You Looked with Your Heart?

Void of place
time and space
an endless merry go round
warpless bounds
black and white
dark and light
beacon of color
lost in spite.

Indescribable

When words fail
and my mind can't comprehend,
you are still good.
When I put you first,
when I put you last,
you love me the same.
You guide my blind heart,
hold my teetering hand,
you never let me go,
I am safe inside your hands.
I fall down,
I push you away,
though you always stay lord,
I'm forever in your grace.
The world shakes me
life throws me around
but the rock on which I stand
shall never move from its ground.
My sovereign redeemer,
you never let me go.

Just Begin

It's been so long since I've picked up a pen.
To move, I realize
I must begin again.

(g)r (o)wh

You can feel it in your heart,
somewhere in your soul
you've learned now,
it's time to let go.
It's time to move forward,
one day at a time,
leaving the parts
you've grown out of behind
it's time to move on now,
it's time to let go.
It's time to keep going,
it's time to grow.

Hidden

Perhaps you might know
perhaps you never will
the keepsake box in my beating chest
has letters for you,
all left unread
you entered my life
wrote your name on my heart
you did this all without notice
oblivious from the start.
And I love you more,
I love you still
the traces of this pen,
where I told you how I feel.
But when you read this
you'll be too late
and that's okay, but know
I still keep you hidden inside my poetry.

Losing Direction

My heart is a maze
an endless road to you
get lost in my mind,
I'll get lost in yours, too.
Your gaze fixed on light
your heart set for love
there's no place you haven't been,
reality's too much
escaping from the ground below
skies blue above,
take me on all your adventures,
make me fall in love.

The Waiting

The hands of time call your name,
patience perfecting fall
I'll wait, I'll wait, I'll wait, I'll wait
I'll wait to give you my all
when you come
the tide will too
the sun will set
and I will move
a place untouched
a place unseen
yet don't overlook
undeniable scenery
the beauty is astounding,
my heart is open wide,
I see the light peeking through the cracks
I see my fears fully being left behind.

Have You Been Hurt?

How do you move on from someone who was never
yours?
One you saw as a friend,
never to be something more?
In my heart,
only you'll understand.
and only you can mend what's left at hand.
But my heart has been broken,
you left it here, open.

Have you been hurt?
Your name comes to mind.

In the Midst —

I need the kind of love
you want to give
maybe I'll learn
to take some of what I give
cried a hundred times,
just to equal this?
Head in the clouds, heart in the midst.

See Through

You have life,
and I do too.
I understand if I'm too busy for you.
But I'd make time,
I'd see through.
That's the difference between me and you.
I'll give you time, I'll give you space
but the longer the clock ticks,
the more thoughts I think.
If you wanted to, you would
if you needed to, you could.
Leave it alone
leave it be
pretending to see
you're not mine to need.

Remains of You

When bones grow old
ashes to stone –
the words remain,
no matter the age.
As time goes on
stories unfold –
the letters in ink,
they shimmer like gold.
Share it now,
share the truth,
beyond the lines you've drawn,
your words still belong to you.

Seeds

Your unlocked potential is vast at sea
effervescent in light
always seeking, planting seeds.

Surrender

I
don't
have
any
words
so
I
lift
my
hands
to
heaven
and
feel
you
read
my
heart.

.

Gaze

So encompassed by you,
I see nothing else.
take not just actions,
but all my thoughts, motives, and reactions.
Mold them for you, to reflect every heartbeat you have.
Let it not be my mind,
but my heart, body, and soul.
Let my eyes look through your lens,
let my feet be set on your path.

A Letter

Tell me how to move on when I was never stuck. I was in no way drawn until you came back. We departed, we said goodbye. When you appeared, so did everything I once felt. And I'm writing this now because I want to let go, but I can't.

Not without letting you know.

I felt then how I feel now. And I don't deserve this, I know. It doesn't make it easier. I tried to be there and you pushed me away, you moved on and now I'm in the way. Everything I thought has changed, who you are now is not who you were then.

So don't come up to me, acting alright – when this whole time we've been anything but fine.

I can't let you go if you continue to stay,
my heart it attached, no matter what I do
if you'll be here, I'll be there waiting for you.

Moments Like This

Coffee drives,
eyes alive
midnight hour,
rainy showers
cafe talks,
morning walks
careless dancing,
mindless planning
car rides,
hearts combined.

Distance

You think I'm far from you,
when distance was never about proximity.

Let Love

Love is an action, yes.
Love cannot solely depend on your feelings.
I'm learning with every day.
This unhealthy give and take,
blurred assumptions have led us to a place without grace.
I'm tired of fighting,
tension in every perfectly placed word.
I've been treading on.
then I remember I don't love for myself,
I don't love to be right,
I don't love for feelings.
I love because love was shown to me first –
and that love has covered me enough.
More than enough.
So I don't have to fight. I simply have to let that love fight
for me.

PART FOUR

BLOOM

My Poetry

I can remember where
I wrote that poem for you.
A late Friday afternoon,
the counter of the coffee shop,
my drink being made by the sweet barista.
And for you,
I laid on my floor,
crying because I couldn't take it anymore.
The night I wanted to last forever,
the night I couldn't wait to forget.
I wrote for hours and hours.
the morning the earth made sure
I felt every afternoon breeze and watched every leaf fall,
I wrote endlessly.
The car ride sunset
that made me think of you,
I scribbled to make sure I remembered that feeling.
You see,
all my life is in my poetry.

Thoughts

Ashamed to admit

my late-night thoughts consist of how you think of me.

How do you see me?

Do you view me in your light?

Do you wonder how my mind works?

What I'm doing tomorrow night?

Do you see me as a fake, an attention-seeking flake?

Or someone to admire,

do you see my heart at stake?

Open Wounds

When you are cut, raw, exposed.
The best time to be shaped –
where your hurt heals from your open wounds.

Someone out There

I have never met someone like you.

your mind is an endless maze I can never find my way around;

every turn is a new wonder.

Your eyes melt my heart, and when the sun shines on them;

there's something I cannot contain.

The way your heart speaks, like it's carrying the loveliest words

to express to me.

I want to be someone you've never met.

One Day

One day, I woke up.
My songs became a little sadder,
my emotions a little deeper.
My thoughts a little heavier,
my days a little busier.
My innocence a little smaller,
my fights a little madder.
My tears a little harder,
my changes a little bigger.
One day, I grew up.

Underneath

Passion
is
lost,
I
cannot
see.
The
pale
point
of
view
has
taught me to be
okay with ordinary
scared of the unseen
when all along
it's been here,
only underneath.

Watching

It's not seeing you
that gets me,
it's watching you leave.

All of You

Take my heart
rid me of my sin
everything I am
all is for you
only you, all of you.
Your grace abounds
your beauty astounds
I want you
only you, all of you.
I will refill
these gaps I've let form
I know you cover me
you're always beside me
so to you,
I let my soul pour out
to you
I let my words cry out
I want you
only you, all of you.

The Meeting

Why can't I see what I continue to need?
I'm confused to say the least,
the more I look
the less I see.
Why do I keep putting my worth
in people who don't know me?
I'm fighting for love I know I won't get
undeserved and ingenuine is all that it is
the sense of being too much
yet not enough
meets me in every way.

Circles

I'm sorry I've been so far
I'm trying to regain who I am
I'm losing myself day by day
it's taken everything in me
not to go insane
who am I?
Who have I become?
I can't feel it anymore
everything is numb
turn and run
run and run
circles I've formed
boundlessly begun.

More Than I See

Because I'm more than hoping you can understand the
depths and widths of
everything I feel because there's no way I could
comprehend it enough to explain it to you myself.

Changing Seasons

This season in my life is one I never want to see pass. Tears on this paper as I'm writing it out. You see, I'm not ready for goodbyes, see-you-laters that will never be. It's only ever been us, now it's just me. And I can fight it or hate it or cry all I want, but at some point we have to let go. We have to move on.

Someone New

All those late-night calls,
all those laughter fits,
all those sweetly sound memories, nearly missed.
I shouldn't wish for it back
all the times you treated me bad
but the fondness I had
to the earlier you
the you you are now
is someone completely new.

Golden Age

You see,
it's not that easy for me
moving on, letting go
the time we've spent and the person I've come to know
you made me as blue as the sky but as
bright as the sun
the times we spent talking, the hours unsung
I miss the days of you and me,
the mellow days lived in simplicity
no blurry fights or dark nights
we were shining bright –
it was the golden age.

Missing

Have you seen her?
She is kind
she is loving
her smile is radiant, her heart is soft
she can lift any spirit, light and darkness
her presence is joyous, her laughter is contagious
her beauty is far beyond looks –
she sees the world in multicolor –
an array, a masterpiece.

Broken

I hope you know that you missed a step.
That you lost something;
and I tried to get it back.
So move on,
that's okay.
And if you come back, I'm sure you can find me.
I forgive you.
I love you.
But you broke me.
You tore at me day after day
you left a tattered mess.
So you'll see me,
but never as close as you once did.

Listen to What Speaks

Let go of the idea you had
the vision
the hold of the past
it's harder to do
easier to say
the memories you have
belong to yesterday
what you have now
is everything you need
lean in closely
everything in your life,
everything you have
speaks.

Wonder

Encompass
surround my space
be my air
let me not spend a second
without you near
take me to your wonder
the valleys of beauty
and rivers of mercy
take me to your heart
the ever-present outpour of grace
surround me everyday
every second I breathe
with all that I behold,
encompass me.

Stigma

Stepping into a new year
I still feel the same
no drastic difference
it's my mind that has to change.

From Dust

And now,
I understand.
I've been broken into a
million pieces,
day by day.
Shattered and torn,
broken and worn.
And slowly,
ever so,
you're beautifully
picking up the pieces
making me whole.

A Broken Record

All we are is a
broken record
ever so gently
we lay on the turntable
and the needle skips
as the music starts
round and round we go,
stuck on repeat.

Real Rest

Perhaps
this season
my hands aren't meant to write
as much as my ears need to listen.
Perhaps
my schedule isn't supposed to be booked
so I can find the meaning of rest
perhaps
my mouth should close
so I can see all the blessings myself
perhaps
this season is for growth.

Your Children

Abba,
your people.
I love your children.
their laughter,
their faces,
their hugs,
their jokes,
their tears,
their smiles,
their dances,
their personality,
their character,
their love,
their grace,
their thoughts,
their questions,
their minds,
their heart for you.

Let Them Free

It is so easy to
sit comfortably in your own thoughts.
be bold enough to let others hear them.

I'm Tired

I'm tired of thinking till I can't feel;
I'm tired of feeling till I can't think.

The Thief

I've never known loneliness
like I know it now
for we are best friends;
him and I
he crept to my door
knocked softly
and I hesitantly let him inside
day by day
week by week
the togetherness of my heart
began to tremble,
but he locked the door
before I could run out
now I don't know where to find the key,
he said it's somewhere inside me.

Who Is She

And what has become of me now? Where do I stand?
I thought I knew myself; that this was where life was
headed,
but right now, I'm not so sure. no, I'm not sure at all.
All these people have left,
but who have they left?
Was it who I used to be?
The me now is someone I'm trying desperately
to figure out, but she won't let me inside.
She is living in the dark crevices of her heart
and desperately wants to seek the light;
but lowers when it begins to find her.
She doesn't want to be found out.
And so she goes, deeper and deeper in the nooks,
finding the depths to her despair and confusion and
withdrawal.
By now, it seemed, she'd find her way out, but the merry-
go-round
in her mind won't let her off. So here she is,
waiting for the ride to stop,
not knowing when it will be.

I Can See It

I see past the comments you make, the jokes you push
aside
I see past the unbothered look, which is really just a lie.
I see past you,
I see who you are
so I don't understand
can you please let down your guard?
You don't have to act like you don't care,
no one is asking you to be tough.
Can you let somebody in to see,
would that ever be enough?

Grace

I was dust
crafted into breath
life in my lungs
I will never forget
once in bondage
touched by the son
living in freedom
my chains are undone
grace outpoured
grace undeserved
grace upon grace
grace forevermore.

Boundary

I know you're probably trying to call my phone;
I already turned it off.
this nightly conversation;
it has to come to a stop.
I can't trick myself and wonder how I feel –
the more I'm around you the more it becomes real.
To hurt you is the last thing I want to do,
but I can't control how you react.
So please don't give me your heart
if you don't want it back.

Lies I Tend to Believe

You'll never be a writer
you don't know what you want
you can't master simple skills?
You'll never amount to much.
There's too many ahead
too many of a kind
you have nothing good to write about
no one cares about your mind
it won't sustain, you can't do it.
You don't have the capacity, it's all an excuse.

Moonlight

Lowlight
sunburn playing softly
pillow resting
lavender scented
candle embers
flame on flame
no noise but
simple tunes
evening moon
glowing sweetly onto you.

How Poetic

How poetic
we came together
as we fell apart
the sun shone brighter
as we became dark
and how I love you
and how I hate you
it's ripping at the seams, this tear between you and me.

Overseas

They said things would change,
I didn't believe them.
but your countless glances, hugs, and smiles
I fell without knowing I've been here for a while.
But that was across the seas, a million miles away.
Now we're back home and everything has changed.

Where I Find You

I have to see if I hear you in my poetry.

You

Falling uncontrollably;
falling for you.

Sleepless

I have no idea what to do
every time I close my eyes
I think of you.
and I wonder, miles away,
if you're staring at your ceiling
thinking of me too.

But You Broke My Heart

I imagined you reading this,
and opening your heart.
listening to all my music,
attentive from the very start
I imagined you meeting my family
and them loving you so,
I imagined taking random trips to places we don't even
know
I imagined us watching my favorite movies,
cliché and romantic as such
I imagined holding your hand
until gravity becomes too much
I imagined windows down and sunny days
making memories we could never replace.
I imagined being slow with this love,
letting the stars align
I imagined midnight dances,
the rain falling just right.

Tell Me

Tell me how to feel
tell me what to do
if you don't give me direction
I'll end up in love with you.

Safe

It's better this way
left in my own resolves
I'm a walking hurricane, I never settle down
I never know what I want and you don't deserve that
I don't wanna think of you
I don't want to know if you're thinking of me
it's easier this way
our hearts aren't in the line of fire, they're tucked away safe.

I Love You

I love you.
I love your smile, and your silly little laugh.
I love the way you look at me and pretend
to be mad.
I love your selflessness and your heart to be kind.
I love how you hand reaches out and gently touches mine.
I love how we got close, so
Unexpected and sweet.
I love how every day you remind me I'm good at being
me.
I love your hugs that I wish would never end, I love your
eyes I always get lost in
And I love that you have no idea this is about you.

Anxiety

Running, running in my head
Never-ending,
beginning again
count to four;
do it again
replay and record
rewind fast forward
ponder and wonder
until your brain hurts.

Porto

Even though I'm here,
I feel you.

Wandering

And I think I'll go to London,
a change of scenery
back to Porto,
where the sunset follows me
I'll try New York,
with her crowded busy streets
own a little plot of land
in Southern Italy.

For the One Graduating

Before you know it, you'll reach it. The time to say goodbye.

To move on.

To turn the page.

Listen,

it's not the big things you'll remember most.

It's the way you sang in your car before school.

It's the same iced latte you ordered every day before class.

It's exactly where you sat in anatomy.

It's the bell after fourth hour you waited to ring every day.

It's a laughter lunch with your best friends arguing about who's driving.

It's the football game that you stormed the field without a care.

It's getting your first car, and probably wrecking it.

It's saying goodbye to the things you never wanted to,

and hello to the things you never thought you would.

It's the messy, it's the heartbreaking, it's the joyful.

It's anything and everything.

It's the bittersweet.

This is your life now, and this is really and everything that's happened and everyone you met got you to right here, right now.

So what happens next?

What You Deserve

You deserve someone who is sure,
someone who undoubtedly wants to be with you.
Someone who won't make you question every move you make,
you deserve someone who will accept you despite your mistakes.
Someone who wants to spend every second with you and someone who eagerly waits to answer you.
You deserve someone who won't leave you wondering what to do next, and how to get them back.

I Didn't Plan This

Here we go again.
I thought this time things would be different,
I thought this time I would see it through.
But these feelings I have, they don't add up to you.
And I cannot drag you on, that's not what I'll do,
but it's so hard to let go when I feel so many truths.
Protect your heart, guard it against me
if it's supposed to be right, why am I in need?

I'm Sorry

The worst part is –
I want to love you
I want to be yours
I want to this to work
I don't want to break your heart.
But I don't,
I won't,
it doesn't,
and I already have.

Song No. 4

I'm so sorry I had to hurt you
never thought that I would see it through
everything we are and could be
lost, stumbling look at me.
Never thought I would have to let you go
it's not your heart, baby you should know
trying so hard to stop your hurt
maybe I'm making it worse
so let me go, let me out
I don't deserve you we know this now
let me down, let me fall
break my heart and take it all
what's the point of going on with the pain
never wanna play this game
our hearts have been through enough
how to say goodbye to your love?
Maybe I'll write it out
so my words can all come out
falling through the sky like rain
my tears will do the same
so let me go let me out
I don't deserve you we know this now

let me down, let me fall
break my heart and take it all.

Higher

Things don't need to make sense
'cause I know where my faith is
and I'll follow you.

Just a Boy

You're just a boy
of course you can't see
the ache inside my soul
it's killing me.

Testimony

Black and white
full of noise
my life was empty
days of void
then your melody
your sweet, sweet symphony
lifted my heart to meet yours
now every breath I breathe
all the beauty I see
every part of me,
it's yours.

Easily

Maybe I just wanted to see if
I was worth fighting for to you;
but you let me go effortlessly,
almost easily.

Your Goodbye

Your goodbye
I never thought
soft and sweet
the weight it carried
to be heavy at least
but your goodbye
uncanny it seemed
it didn't matter to you
you were okay to see me leave
no, your goodbye
was not what I thought
unbelief I'd seen
your goodbye
left you sane
still with a part of me.

Watch It Illuminate

Falling in love with life;
what a beautiful thing.
watching the sun rise, the glistening peak of a new day
filling the in-betweens with lovely to-dos,
fueled by purpose
wrapped in joy
they say falling in love is something you can't control
and I almost agree
I've fallen in love with life
it's taken ahold of me.

Something

I feel a distance between you and I;
something I can't replace
what's separating us is scary;
something I can't explain
even worse it's weariness;
something I can't control
but we trudge on;
something I can't let go of.

Everything I Learned

His words knew exactly where to start the fire,
where to light the match.
Me, on the other hand, felt understood
I was considered a darkened map.
But when the flames drew close and you started to burn –
you only loved me with your words (is everything I
learned).

Alleluia

I am mourned for what I don't have
mourned for what I do
I muttered the words,
"You have my heart,"
as I lost it to you
found what I lost
lost what I knew
when I gave you my heart
you made it completely new
drew my mind
whispered in truth
words I never heard before
all unseen before you
start and end
beginning to finish
this working of my heart
before I even took a breath
and what I lost
is nothing
compared to
what I have found.

Surrender

You know my heart
you know it best.
It's a daily choice to forget the rest.
The fear, the unknown
doubt and uncertainty
when I least have the strength,
and in my weakness
there you'll be.

Who You Are

I know you want to run away
to go somewhere new
but right here,
in the mundane
this is where he needs you.
you are not overlooked.
You are not unseen.
You are loved and you are known
by the king of kings.

Still Blooming

You are making a poem out of me
one that carefully crafts your love
in eloquent words
equally messy, ones that have been hurt
words that have been shown mercy through the hard times
ones shown grace.
ones that take every syllable
and form them to your perfect face.
The struggles, the highs
the falls and the flys
all of them written out –
all of them brought to life
a life full of you and all it's meant to be –
yes, here you are
making a poem out of me.

keep blooming